BALLPARK LEGENDS

The Legacy of the Negro Leagues

Elliott Smith
Cicely Lewis, Executive Editor

Lerner Publications ◆ Minneapolis

LETTER FROM CICELY LEWIS

Dear Reader,

When you think of today's star Black athletes, who comes to mind? Maybe you think of LeBron James, Mookie Betts, Dak Prescott, or Simone Biles. They are all great athletes. But do you know who paved the way for them?

Cicely Lewis

I began Read Woke Books to challenge social norms and to share stories of people from underrepresented and oppressed groups. In this series, you will be introduced to lesser-known athletes and the barriers they overcame to make great changes in sports.

Sports is more than a game. Throughout history, sports have been a way to help fight injustices in our world. As you read, think about how the actions athletes have made in their sports have impacted the world.

I hope these books inspire you to never give up. Someone has to take the first step, and it might as well be you.

Power to the Reader,

Cicely Lewis, Executive Editor

TABLE OF CONTENTS

FORGOTTEN FIRST 4

CHAPTER 1
THE BEGINNINGS 6

CHAPTER 2
PLAYING THEIR WAY 12

CHAPTER 3
SUPERSTARS 18

CHAPTER 4
LEGACY AND FUTURE 23

Glossary 28
Source Notes 29
Read Woke Reading List 30
Index 31

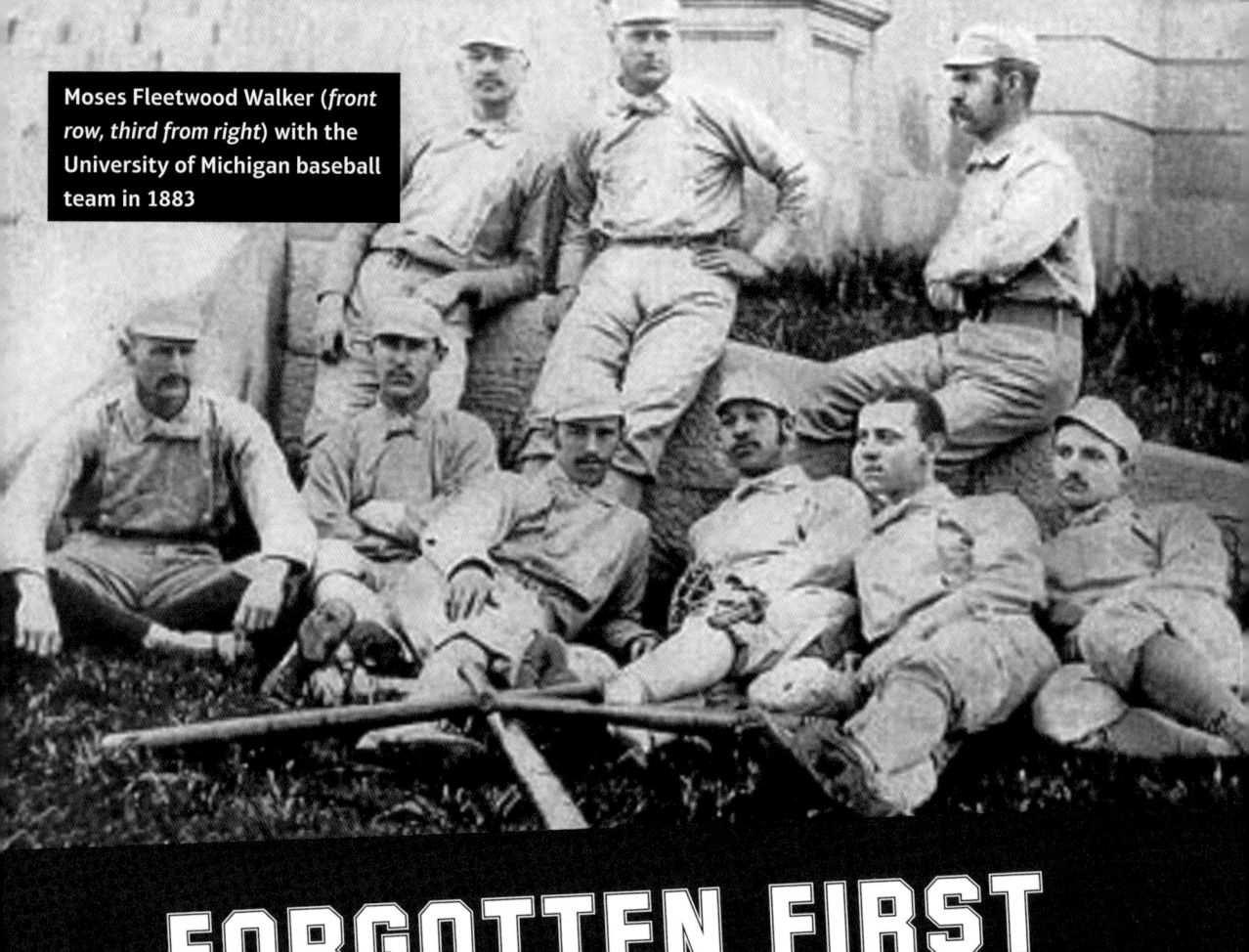

Moses Fleetwood Walker (*front row, third from right*) with the University of Michigan baseball team in 1883

FORGOTTEN FIRST

Baseball became popular in the United States in the late 1800s. Even though Black players sometimes played on all-white teams for one game, teams were segregated. Moses Fleetwood Walker changed that. Walker was a catcher at the University of Michigan. In 1883 he left school to play for the Toledo Blue Stockings, a minor-league team.

When the Blue Stockings joined the American Association in 1884, Walker became the first Black major-league player. It was difficult for Walker on and off the field. Catching was a tough position. Catchers did not use a glove, or any chest or leg protection. Walker was often injured. He faced racism from fans, opponents, and even his own teammates. After the 1884 season, the Blue Stockings released Walker.

Then, in 1887, baseball owners made a secret agreement not to sign any new Black players. It would be more than 60 years before another Black player returned to the majors.

But that didn't mean the game was over for Black players. The story of the Negro Leagues was just beginning.

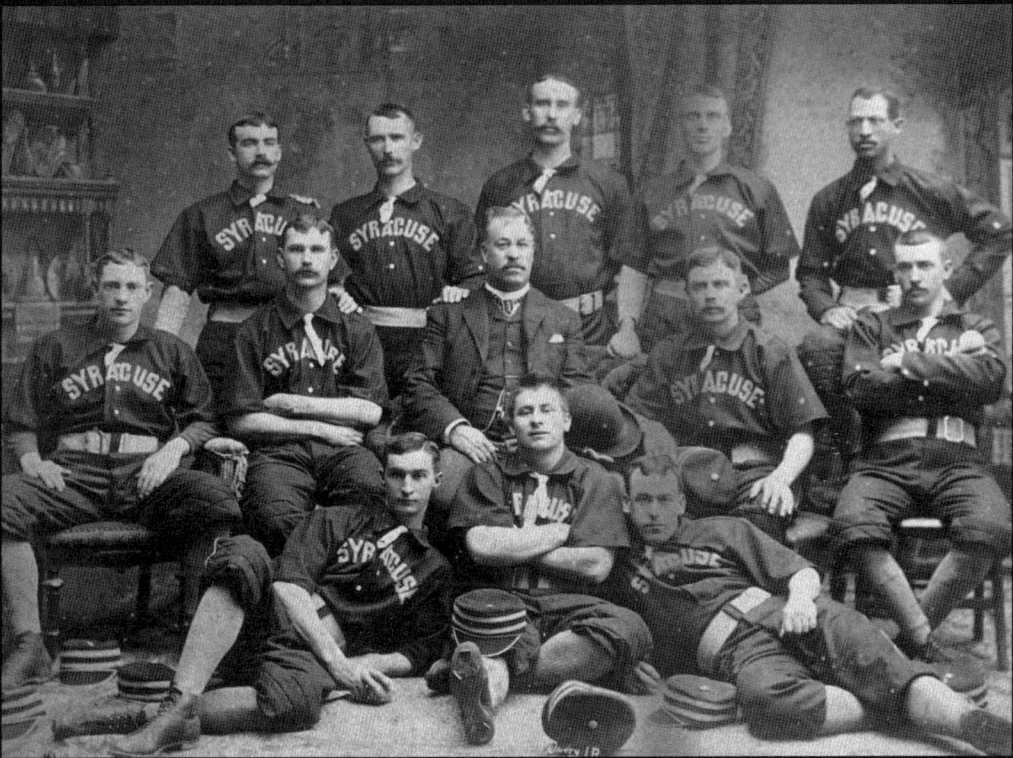

Walker (*back row, right*) in 1889 with the minor-league Syracuse Stars

The Baltimore Blues, pictured here in 1890, were an early all-Black team in Baltimore, Maryland.

CHAPTER 1
THE BEGINNINGS

The major leagues had banned Black players. But that didn't stop Black players from forming their own teams. Black teams didn't have their own stadiums. But they were loaded with talent. They traveled across the country to take on anyone who would play them. This was called barnstorming.

Teams such as the Philadelphia Pythians played other Black teams including the Bachelor Club of Albany and the Mutuals of Washington, DC. They also played against some white teams in exhibition games. These integrated games mostly

REFLECT

The term Negro is rarely used today because of its racist history. But it is used proudly when discussing the baseball leagues. Why do you think that is the case?

took place in the North and Midwest. But some barnstorming teams played games in Canada and Mexico.

By 1920 some players and owners wanted to better organize Black baseball. They turned to former player Rube Foster for help. Foster had dominated opponents as a pitcher. In 1911

Rube Foster in his Leland Giants uniform in 1909

DID YOU KNOW?

Effa Manley was the first woman to join the National Baseball Hall of Fame. She co-owned the Newark Eagles from 1935 to 1948 and was a powerful advocate for Black baseball.

Effa Manley in the Eagles' dugout in 1948

he formed the Chicago American Giants. The team was so popular that it often had more fans than the Cubs and the White Sox, Chicago's major-league teams.

Foster argued for a pro Black league. But both owners and players were used to barnstorming. They were afraid of losing their independence. Foster convinced people of his vision. In 1920 the Negro National League formed. The first set of teams were in Chicago, Cincinnati, Dayton (Ohio), Detroit, Indianapolis, Kansas City, and St. Louis.

The early success of the league led to other pro leagues such as the Southern Negro League and Eastern Colored League. The best teams in the leagues faced each other at the end of the season in the Negro League World Series.

The Chicago American Giants, shown here in 1922, won the first three Negro National League championships.

> "As a child, my dream was to be a part of black baseball. Back then, black children had limited access to sports. . . . We took advantage of every opportunity we had, and black baseball was one."
>
> —Wilmer Fields, Negro League pitcher and outfielder

Players pose for a group photo at the 1936 Negro League All-Star Game at Comiskey Park in Chicago

The 1935 Pittsburgh Crawfords won the Negro National League.

It was not easy for many teams. Travel was difficult. Players would leave town just as quickly as they arrived. Teams often went out of business with little warning. The Great Depression, a time of worldwide economic hardship, began in 1929. It hit baseball hard. The Negro National League stopped play in 1931. Two years later, Pittsburgh Crawfords owner Gus Greenlee restarted the league. Then, in 1937, the Negro American League formed. This league became the home for many of the game's stars.

Josh Gibson slides into home during the 1944 East-West All-Star Game, helping the West win 7–4.

CHAPTER 2
PLAYING THEIR WAY

The game in the Negro Leagues looked a lot different from Major League Baseball (MLB). In the major leagues, power was key to success. Teams relied on sluggers such as Babe Ruth to hit home runs. The Negro Leagues also had its share of home run hitters. But it had its own style.

Speed was key to success for many Negro League teams. Bunting, stealing, and aggressive baserunning were important. Players never slid into bases headfirst. Instead, they slid feetfirst so the metal spikes on their shoes would make it difficult for fielders to tag them.

Pitchers kept hitters on their toes. Leon Day of the Newark Eagles used a no-windup pitch, which made the ball hard to track. George Harney used spitballs and sandpaper-scraped balls to keep hitters off-balance. These pitches were not

Satchel Paige throws a pitch before a game against the New York Yankees in 1948.

allowed, but Negro League umpires often didn't enforce the rule. Satchel Paige had many pitches that he called by unique names, such as the Trouble Ball and Long Tom.

Negro League play was fast and fun, and crowds loved it. Teams such as the Indianapolis Clowns played to the audience. They sometimes turned games into a show with ball tricks, juggling, and dancing on the field.

Fans watch a Negro League game at Forbes Field in Pittsburgh.

DID YOU KNOW?

Pittsburgh was home to the first Black-owned stadium. Greenlee Field opened in 1932 and was home of the Pittsburgh Crawfords until 1938.

Greenlee Field in 1932

DID YOU KNOW?

Jackie Robinson played one season in the Negro Leagues. Then, in 1947, Robinson joined the Brooklyn Dodgers. He was the first Black player in MLB.

Robinson takes the field in a 1951 game for the Dodgers.

The 1930 St. Louis Stars included great players such as Mule Suttles (*top left*), Cool Papa Bell (*bottom, fourth from right*), and Willie Wells (*top, second from left*).

    The Negro Leagues were full of firsts. Newark Eagles shortstop and third baseman Willie Wells was the first player to wear protective headgear while hitting. Wells was struck by a pitch in the head in 1936. The next day he played wearing a type of hard hat. Other players soon followed. MLB players didn't start wearing batting helmets until 1941, and it wasn't required until 1971.

    Other firsts for the Negro Leagues included expanded protective gear for catchers and night baseball games. The first game under the lights was hosted by the Kansas City Monarchs in 1930. Night games allowed fans to come to the park after they were done working for the day.

Paige throws a pitch for the St. Louis Browns in the early 1950s.

CHAPTER 3
SUPERSTARS

Some of the greatest players in the history of baseball played in the Negro Leagues. Still, many remain largely unknown to baseball fans. If Black players had been allowed to play in the major leagues from the beginning, they could have written a different kind of legacy.

Different rules, styles of play, and playing conditions make it hard to compare MLB and Negro League players. The majors kept stats on players and games that help tell its history. But Negro League games rarely had official scorers—people who

REFLECT

Some Negro League players remained loyal to the leagues even after Jackie Robinson opened the doors to MLB. Why do you think a player would choose to stay in the Negro Leagues?

recorded stats at baseball games. Satchel Paige claimed to have pitched in more than 2,500 games. But there's no way to prove it because of the lack of official records. Paige is one of the biggest names in Negro League history. He had a name for each of his pitches, such as Bee Ball and Midnight Creeper. He would call in his fielders, make them sit down, and then strike out the next three hitters. He went from team to team to make more money.

Josh Gibson was a great slugger in the Negro Leagues. He hit huge home runs and was a great catcher. James Thomas "Cool Papa" Bell was among the fastest baseball players ever.

> "I played with Willie Mays and against Hank Aaron. They were tremendous players, but they were no Josh Gibson."
> —Monte Irvin, Negro League outfielder

Catcher Josh Gibson was one of the greatest sluggers in Negro League history.

Cool Papa Bell

Buck Leonard

First baseman Walter "Buck" Leonard was also a great hitter. Thousands of players made an impact on the sport, many of whom have been forgotten.

Women also played a role in the Negro Leagues. In the 1950s, Toni Stone became the first woman to join a Negro League team. She played second base for the Indianapolis Clowns. In 50 games that season, she batted .243. Some reports say she even hit a single off of Paige.

After Stone left the team, the Clowns signed two more women. Connie Morgan took over Stone's spot at second base. Mamie "Peanut" Johnson became the first female pitcher in the Negro Leagues. She threw a mix of curves, sliders, and screwballs.

Toni Stone of the Indianapolis Clowns in 1953

REFLECT

The women who played Negro League baseball often faced discrimination from players, fans, and even their teammates. Why do you think Black men would discriminate even as they were being barred from playing in the majors?

Hank Aaron started his career in the Negro Leagues, then went on to break Babe Ruth's career home run record in MLB. He's shown here with the Braves in 1954.

CHAPTER 4
LEGACY AND FUTURE

When MLB integrated in 1947, it was the beginning of the end for the Negro Leagues. The best young Black players began making their way to the majors. Players such as Hank Aaron and Willie Mays, who started in the Negro Leagues, became MLB legends. But it wasn't easy. Black players continued to face racism in the big leagues for decades.

With star players gone, attendance for Negro League games dropped and teams were losing money. By 1960 the last few teams folded. Black baseball was a thing of the past.

For years, the glory of the Negro Leagues faded away. But in 1971 Satchel Paige became the first Negro League player to join the Hall of Fame. More Negro League legends joined in the following years.

In 1971 Paige became the first Negro League player to join the Hall of Fame.

The Negro Leagues Baseball Museum is filled with displays that honor the Negro Leagues.

In the decades that followed, baseball experts researched the lost history of the Negro Leagues. Stories of amazing players, fantastic feats, and lost opportunities due to racism shed new light on a nearly forgotten era of baseball.

Buck O'Neil was a first baseman and manager for the Kansas City Monarchs. In 1962 he became the first Black coach in the major leagues. O'Neil became one of the best spokespeople for the Negro Leagues. He played a big role in the creation of the Negro Leagues Baseball Museum in Kansas City in 1990.

The museum is home to many objects from the Negro Leagues era. The museum has been so popular that in 2023 it announced plans to use $25 million to grow.

In December 2020, MLB announced that the seven Negro Leagues would be moved to major-league status. Player stats would count in the official record books.

In 2023 the Negro Leagues entered the spotlight again. The video game *MLB The Show 23* created a Negro Leagues story mode. Players of the video game can learn more about this important era of baseball. The game gave young fans a chance to connect with many of history's forgotten greats.

For decades, the players of the Negro Leagues were largely ignored. But slowly, that's changing. More and more fans have the chance to appreciate Negro League players' contributions to the game.

> "[The inclusion of Negro League stats] serves as historical validation for those who had been shunned from the Major Leagues and had the foresight and courage to create their own league that helped change the game and our country too."
>
> —Bob Kendrick, president of the Negro Leagues Baseball Museum, 2020

REFLECT

For decades, the number of Black players in the major leagues has been declining. Many top Black athletes choose to play sports such as football and basketball instead. What do you think Negro League stars would say about this?

Minnesota Twins outfielder Byron Buxton rounds third in a game against the Kansas City Royals in 2023.

GLOSSARY

advocate: to publicly support something and work toward advancing it

barnstorm: to travel through the country making brief stops for games

bunt: a baseball play in which a batter turns his bat and tries to poke the ball into the infield

discriminate: to deny one opportunities based on a characteristic such as race or gender

exhibition: a game that doesn't count in official standings or records

integrate: to make a place or job open to all racial and ethnic groups

official scorer: a person who records statistics at a baseball game

segregate: a legal system of forced separation, done specifically by race

stats: short for statistics, the numerical values of one's performance

SOURCE NOTES

10 Wilmer Fields, *My Life in the Negro Leagues: An Autobiography*, McLean, VA: Miniver, 2013, xiii.

19 David Schoenfield, "Ten Greatest Negro Leaguers," *ESPN*, February 24, 2015, https://www.espn.com/blog/sweetspot/post/_/id/55331/ten-greatest-negro-leaguers-of-all-time.

26 "MLB Officially Designates the Negro Leagues as 'Major League,'" MLB.com, December 16, 2020, https://www.mlb.com/press-release/press-release-mlb-officially-designates-the-negro-leagues-as-major-league.

READ WOKE READING LIST

Britannica Kids: Negro Leagues
https://kids.britannica.com/students/article/Negro-leagues/632863

MLB: The Negro Leagues
https://www.mlb.com/history/negro-leagues

National Baseball Hall of Fame
https://baseballhall.org

Negro Leagues Baseball Museum
https://www.nlbm.com

Smith, Elliott. *Black Achievements in Sports: Celebrating Fritz Pollard, Simone Biles, and More*. Minneapolis: Lerner Publications, 2024.

Weatherford, Carole Boston. *A Negro League Scrapbook*. New York: Astra Young Readers, 2022.

Williams, Andrea. *Baseball's Leading Lady: Effa Manley and the Rise and Fall of the Negro Leagues*. New York: Roaring Brook, 2021.

INDEX

Aaron, Hank, 19, 23

Foster, Rube, 7, 9

Gibson, Josh, 19
Greenlee Field, 15

Indianapolis Clowns, 14, 21

Manley, Effa, 8
Mays, Willie, 19, 23
MLB The Show 23, 26

National Baseball Hall of Fame, 8, 24
Negro American League, 11
Negro Leagues Baseball Museum, 25–26
Negro National League, 9, 11

O'Neil, Buck, 25

Paige, Satchel, 14, 19, 21, 24

Robinson, Jackie, 16, 19

Stone, Toni, 21

Walker, Moses Fleetwood, 4–5

PHOTO ACKNOWLEDGMENTS

Image credits: Cicely Lewis portrait photos by Fernando Decillis, p. 2; Historic Images/Alamy, p. 4; Transcendental Graphics/Getty Images, pp. 5, 6, 8, 9, 17, 22; Chicago History Museum/Getty Images, p. 7; Heritage Auctions/Wikimedia Commons (PD), p. 10; RLPM Collection/Alamy, pp. 11, 21; Bettmann/Getty Images, p. 12; Archive Photos/Stringer/Getty Images, p. 13; Teenie Harris Archive/Carnegie Museum of Art/Getty Images, pp. 14, 15; Keystone/Stringer/Getty Images, p. 16; New York Times Co./Getty Images, p. 18; AP Photo, pp. 20, 23; Smith Archive/Alamy, p. 24; ZUMA Press, Inc./Alamy, p. 25; AP Photo/Bruce Kluckhohn, p. 27.

Design elements: Sandipkumar Patel/Getty Images; Colors Hunter/Getty Images.

Cover: RLPM Collection/Alamy; AP Photo.

Copyright © 2025 by Lerner Publishing Group, Inc.

All rights reserved. International copyright secured. No part of this book may be reproduced, stored in a retrieval system, or transmitted in any form or by any means—electronic, mechanical, photocopying, recording, or otherwise—without the prior written permission of Lerner Publishing Group, Inc., except for the inclusion of brief quotations in an acknowledged review.

Lerner Publications Company
An imprint of Lerner Publishing Group, Inc.
241 First Avenue North
Minneapolis, MN 55401 USA

For reading levels and more information, look up this title at www.lernerbooks.com.

Main body text set in Aptifer Sans LT Pro.
Typeface provided by Linotype AG.

Editor: Matt Doeden **Designer:** Viet Chu **Photo Editor:** Nicole Berglund
Lerner team: Martha Kranes

Library of Congress Cataloging-in-Publication Data

Names: Smith, Elliott, 1976– author.
Title: Ballpark legends : the legacy of the Negro Leagues / Elliot Smith.
Description: Minneapolis : Lerner Publications, [2024] | Series: Read Woke Books. Black trailblazers in sports | Includes bibliographical references and index. | Audience: Ages 9–14 years | Audience: Grades 4–6 | Summary: "From the late 1800s to 1947, Major League Baseball prevented Black athletes from competing. Many played in the Negro Leagues. Learn about the history of the Negro Leagues and some of baseball's greatest players"— Provided by publisher.
Identifiers: LCCN 2023043858 (print) | LCCN 2023043859 (ebook) | ISBN 9798765611548 (library binding) | ISBN 9798765628492 (paperback) | ISBN 9798765632680 (epub)
Subjects: LCSH: Negro leagues—History—Juvenile literature. | African American baseball players—Juvenile literature. | Major League Baseball (Organization)—Juvenile literature. | Baseball—United States—History—Juvenile literature.
Classification: LCC GV875.A1 S575 2024 (print) | LCC GV875.A1 (ebook) | DDC 796.357/640973—dc23/eng/20231124

LC record available at https://lccn.loc.gov/2023043858
LC ebook record available at https://lccn.loc.gov/2023043859

Manufactured in the United States of America
1-1010004-51776-12/7/2023